Emergence

Writings by the JHCC Writers Guild

MONGREL EMPIRE PRESS
NORMAN, OKLAHOMA, UNITED STATES OF AMERICA

2019

FIRST EDITION, 2019

Emergence: Writings by the JHCC Writers Guild
© 2019 The JHCC Writers Guild Authors

ISBN 978-1-7323935-5-4

Cover Image:
© Rico Cruz

MONGREL EMPIRE PRESS
NORMAN, OK

ONLINE CATALOGUE: WWW.MONGRELEMPIRE.ORG

This publisher is a proud member of

COUNCIL OF LITERARY MAGAZINES & PRESSES
W W W . C L M P . O R G

Contents

Acknowledgements for the Emergence

JHCC Writers Guild

No work would be finished or legitimate without first giving honor to whom it is due. The Writers Guild was established in March 2016 by a handful of inmates, some of whom remain active members. In October 2017, author and Executive Director of OK Message Project Cheri Fuller introduced University of Oklahoma professors Michele Eodice, Nick LoLordo, Catherine Mintler, and Rachel Jackson to the Guild who took an immediate liking to them. Other professors have since joined their ranks. These men and women dedicate countless hours and dollars in support of us and our vision. They have taught and mentored, encouraged and criticized with love and compassion. We are an extremely diverse group of men (as you will see in the following pages), all with our own talents and baggage. But these volunteers embrace us as artists, writers and most importantly human beings. To them we are eternally grateful.

The Emergence is but a small glimpse, a primary glance, at the depth and breadth of the men contained in its covers. We are passion. We are timidity. We are courage. We are hilarity. We are smooth operators penning fibs filled with verity. We are oxymorons and quintessential examples; we are more than a handful. Gird up your loins and prepare for mental insurgence . . . now presenting the Emergence!

RENGA

Blind spots exist in
The peripheral caverns
Of a dream chaser

Yet he continues to run
Determination his fuel

Sometimes life's brush paints
With the most cruel of colors;
A grotesque art form

Depending on the person
The brushstroke of life differs

Tunnel vision dreams
Narrow the peripheral view
Of the picture

Visualizing my dreams
Pleasant images of life

Words spoken may say
Opposite of the meaning
Can the truth be proof

Human origin. Red dirt
Words planted in our heart grow

Concise truth takes form
Harvesting a real bounty
The fruit is called love

But beware rot starts within
Slowly eating its way out

Lies can kill love
Perforating all levels
Cancerous filth

A myopic view of life
Kills all hope of loving life

Nefarious life
Destroys family and dreams
Righteousness, last chance.

Love God with all your being
And your neighbor as yourself

Truth shall set you free
From blind spots and myopia
Love heals shattered lives

Each generation must choose
How to implement that truth.

The struggle of life
Is a judgment sight unseen
Prepare to face it

At the right revealing point
All our secrets will be judged

What clear perspective
No one is beyond the reach
Of comprehension of death

In agreement with those words
Universal is the truth

So what is life then
Knowing death is for certain
Opportunity

Dying to live in this life
Living to die in the next

Soothing waterfalls
Pleasant paradise eye view
Relaxing clear thoughts

Tranquility smooths the face
Cleansing the soul—life is sweet!

Lovingly peaceful
Fields of hope make freedom real
Time unlocks the door

Time: tool of infinity
It must be handled with care

A man's mind set free—
Like the eyes of an eagle;
Searches most intently.

What always consumes your thoughts
Controls your eye's direction

God is a great force
His love is the continued force
None can reckon with

What is god?
Or should I say who?
For some the answer hurts.

Finding out the truth
Only comes to those who search
Seek and you shall find

To you be your way
And to me be mine
Faith draw the line

Agree to disagree
But is this unity
When we draw the line?

Unity brings harmony
Harmonizing in one voice

Seeking help in life
A mere man with divine gifts
Internally rich

Success is measured by whom?
Failure brings experience

Time will show the path
A journey starts with a step
Weigh the options.

But acknowledge this as well
Life's meant to be lived!!

Who knows how it ends?
One foot after the other . . .
Never look back

Life lived for others is rich
Gifts given become your present

Earth, life's proving station
Eternity lives final stop
Faith, the only answer

The more sweat lost in training,
The less worry in judgment

I want to be well
In my mind, spirit, and soul
And that's a challenge.

ROAD TO REALITY

I
Black folk still dying, police still racist
and the penitentiary is the new form of education;
So buckle up 'cause it's gonna be a long ride
On this road to reality where hate and hope collide.

'Cause . . . somebody lied to you if they said "It's getting better"
The sun IS shining somewhere, but all I see is stormy weather.
An' Stormy . . . well, she never thought she'd get her chance to speak
'bout a hypocrite of a president who's an undercover freak.

Come to think of it, his situation really ain't unique
wit this hush money, them oligarchs, and dead bodies in the street.
N' speaking of streets, why is it mine got to be infected;
filthy needles connect wit black skin filled with every evil you injected;

That includes the one's charged wit keepin' me protected;
I ain't free to take a knee though, but they free to put one off
        in my neck, an' . . .
what the heck ever happened to justice and equality for all
well they say if you lookin' hard enough you'll find that at
        the border wall—
an' who gon' pay for that . . . except for each and every one of y'all.

So while you at it, c'mon, pay attention y'all:
'cause the new way to kill time mean killin' mine for these cops
        wit Black trophies on the walls,
They get away, consequence unseen, which means for us there is
        no *justice*,
just one more reason for us to distrust the upholders of the law.
Even as our people rise, yet another of us fall,
and it's us gettin' chopped like trees,
an' no matter what it seems no amount of money can silence a
        mother's screams.

You can call me a skeptic, but in my mind, man, perhaps
it's no coincidence that legislators and all they taxes
got you unable to pay yo' bills; meanwhile they vacation and relax.

White folk out there screamin' how . . . They takin' Amerikkka back,
'n the only thing Starbucks want in they store is coffee . . . if it's black
So think about that black,
'cause it's you that's in the crosshairs, you that's under attack
Y'all screamin' and hollerin' "Protect ya neck son,"

5

While I'm teachin' my sons to protect they back
that's where the knife gon' be at;
But justice is blind right, so she ain't gon' see that.
It's getting' hard for me to breathe at night, I think I need a C-PAP . . .
n' I really hate to see that . . .

For them, it's comin' together kinda like . . . clutch plates;
meanwhile I'm so hungry for change man, feel like I gotta . . .
    clutch plates,
an' I'm coming to grips wit what it is I really hate.
So I'm just gon' take a moment if I may, to elaborate:
really, what's botherin' me is worse than whites that discriminate,
It's that the Black skin surrounding Black men is what Black women is
    startin' to hate;
Blackness won't survive that fate,
All the while wit a crooked smile, it's a plan the white man initiate, got
    our women takin' the bait;
But is success really success when it's yourself you've come to hate?

That's why . . . Black folks still dyin' . . .

II
    . . . police still racist
and the penitentiary is the new form of education;
So buckle up cause it's gon' be a long ride
on this road to reality where hate and hope collide.

There's unity in equality, it's ours for the taking
but we refuse to grasp the concept, so we take that knife that's in
    nine inches,
pull it out a couple then call it progress.
See, I don't agree with a whole lot and there ain't a whole lot that would
    agree with me,
and every since I was a young pup, I knew it'd get ruff, cuz there's
always a cat tryin' to feed off a dog's pedigree;
My advice? Don't come half-steppin' with me,
so many rats in this race I shoulda invested in cheese;
Rappers selling fairy tales, dummies purchasing dreams,
and since they like to compare life with chess, tell me: who's ready to
    murder their king?
These suckas turnin' tricks for females and bruh, that ain't cool to see,
so when T-lady ask why I sacrificed my queen?
If truth be told, I ain't like her makin' more moves than me;
it ain't cool with me, this penitentiary put up fences that turns
    love into hatred,

6

and since this is chess, I know when I reach the other side, I'll have
    another one waitin'.
Currently I reside in the land of the free where the price of being human
    ain't cheap,
and justice is steep, the land where minorities are gunned down
    every week,
blatantly refusing our civil rights to be equal;
and since niggas hangin' from trees wasn't politically conducive,
they decided to substitute that noose with the needle.

So I'm not proud to be an ameriKKKan;
while I appreciate those who laid down their lives for the freedoms
    to be had,
with that said: obscene gestures to the red white and blue,
with a middle finger for every star on that flag,
"Why?" some would ask, my reply: (I—M Momentum)

Black folks still dying . . .

III
. . . Police still racist,
and the penitentiary is the new form of education;
so buckle up 'cause it's gon' be a long ride
on this road to reality where hate and hope collide.

Because we're who they're training against . . . so of course
    I'm offended,
and they wonder why we stay in offense, 'cause we stay in a fence;
and to get a break depends on the shade of our skin,
and they fake and pretend like we makin' amends,
when we already know they lyin' (lion); and wish they'd stay in that den.
But then again, in prison accomplishments, y'all admire me
    to its entirety,
even go as far as inspiring until I enter society,
where you start denyin' me because of the background you entitled me
now the environment I'm in becomes dangerous . . . not for them
    but for me—
because of how I'm looked at;
then I look back and see the same chains that hooked Blacks,
Well look at that!

Police were supposed to be peacemakers, but instead were
    piece makers
with a badge that gave them authority through empty chambers
    to release anger;
and you can't convince me otherwise,

it'll just be another lie to undermine what's been undisguised . . .
ANOTHER FORM OF RACISM.

And wanna talk down on us 'cause we on welfare, and I don't think
    that's well, fair—
because their neglection of our protection helped us get there.

Now we sent into rage 'cause of minimum wage,
and the money they claimed to be given—
doesn't even matter when they keep raising our standard of living;
I mean, I'm puzzled, that's why I don't try to fit,
because it sucks the life out of me;
these politics are a pile of ticks,
but that's what we get though, for trusting their info,
cause now we got a poverty line, and we below it,
it look like we tryin' to limbo.

And rich folk breakin' necks to see what's breakin' next
while we in the projects wonderin' who gon' break in next!

Na'im, bro, police takin' bets when they pull us over because of our
skin color so remember . . . you not white, yet if you were a bit *Moe
Ghetto*, Na'im, you'd have a Dilemma;

That's why Black folks still dyin' . . .

IV
    . . . Police still racist
and the penitentiary is the new form of education;
So buckle up cause it's gon' be a long ride
on this road to reality where hate and hope collide.

Is this what it's meant to be? Rejected from society,
struggles and poverty; no one predicted such a prophecy.
Since I was conceived, was lead to believe that I was free,
in a country that was based on justice and liberty—
but how could this be?
When I've been cursed since the begin,
labelled minority by the complexion of my skin,
so much oppression we live in,
and every day it increase, what's peace?
I know they'd rather see me dead in the streets
jealousy and envy are reasons why, believe it or not,
if they don't kill me then they devise a plot to keep me on lock.
Stereotyped, labeled and judged before it's known what I'm like;
a fair trial, yeah, that's right, applied only to whites.

That's how it is and how it's been, no need to soften the truth;
and Trump in office is the nail that seals the coffin of proof;
I'm often aloof from politics 'cause I despise politicians,
they only speak of good intentions so the people will listen;
meanwhile conditions for my kind is still the same as they was,
projects and ghettos filled with guns, drugs, gangsters and thugs.
Low income housing, welfare and underfunded education,
results from budget cuts for less important operations.
Now graduation rates for my kind is on the decline,
while incarceration rates have risen and continue to climb;
we live in a time in which it seems we've lived before,
a time where it seems we're headed toward another civil war.
The hypocrisy of democracy is evil in deed
because the people who seek to lead are not the people we need.
Greed and the lust for power the underlying intent;
Republican, Democrat and even Independent.
Regardless what party wins, watch the pattern unfold,
that party's only concerns are its own plans and its goals.
So many lost souls and sick hearts, so much corruption and evil,
because the laws of man have now become the laws of the people.

Destruction and devastation, we ain't fit for legislation;
making laws on top of laws yet it's the lawmakers that break them.
So tell me why I shouldn't hate them? Why not hold a grudge?
I can't show love to people who ain't never showed me no love!
And say what you like, but won't convince me that I'm wrong
        when I'm right;
and we can't get along when you condone what's wrong like it's right.
I've never been white, so I can't tell you what it's like to be that,
been Black since my birth and I prefer to be none other than that.
And his story's wrong, they make it seem like we've been slaves
        all along;
but if you seek you'll find that we been getting played all along.
I prayed for so long until I found how I was praying was wrong,
and I was fooled into thinking I was saved all along.
I know some folks will feel like what I'm saying is wrong,
well, who are they to say what's wrong with what I say in my poem?
Freedom of speech, yet I'm still hated for how freely I speak;
for fear of who my words might reach and give them freedom to think.
When we hear history we mentally grab thoughts from the past;
and presently we overlook the current problems we have.
If not for the mercy of Allah ain't no way we could last,
before too long we will surely be a thing of the past . . . History

Cuz Black folks still dying, police still racist,
and the penitentiary is the new form of education;
So buckle up cause it's gonna be a long ride
on this road to reality where hate and hope collide.

To the reader:

You have just experienced four of JHCC's eight most gifted spoken word artists. We routinely offer any who feel they have the skills to defeat us an opportunity to step forward . . . to date, none have.

We are not idle minds, we are not stereotypes. We are different races. We are intelligent, rational men. We are not simply entertainers, we are activists; we have a message and we will not be silent!

Part I: Shof'tim

Part II: Shannon the Apprehensive

Part III: Dilemma A.K.A. Stroke Game Vicious

Part IV: Anonymous Kquote

MICHAEL "RICO" CRUZ A.K.A. RICH CROSS

I was born in Bronx, N.Y., in December of 1970 and raised by an adolescent single mother and the streets between South Central and San Pedro, California. I believe it would be adequate to say, "I have never met any streets that were kind to my feet." Yet, a difficult life hasn't deterred my love of art. Working in multiple media of drawing and painting and utilizing different techniques, I've thrived in the joy of being free to create.

My writing is semi-autobiographical, using actual and fictionalized events from life to illustrate a philosophy that demonstrates our apparent physical limits are merely appearance.

Generally, my writing tends to betray the ethos I have continued to live throughout my constant pursuit of spiritual growth. Therefore, the genres of writing I have chosen evolve from inspiration of the subjects, which lend themselves to the creative artery of the heart. As I continue to mature into a writer of great heights, I fly with the seagulls until the world recognizes the words of an eagle.

Until then, I am certainly grateful and profoundly humbled by all of the authors who inspire me to climb upon their strong shoulders.

WONDERFUL HAIR: THE BETRAYAL OF MY FOLLICLES

"Hair," Oh where did you go? I wonder

Though the answer escapes me
I begin trying to understand
Why my follicles have betrayed my skin

I look in the mirror at all the hair
And wonder why is it
That my face
Can become a forest with teeth
Yet my head looks like
Something is missing between the trees

Oh "Hair," oh where oh where did you go?
A simple *Hmm* comes to mind
Was it the long days without a wash
That now makes my head glow, like a freshly applied coat of wax!

These are some of the thoughts that come to mind
When some of us shave the remaining limbs
To make us look even in the end
Then again there are those who drag it over to one end

Oh! Hair, when will you start to grow?
Don't you know, you have abandoned your post
And that is what I miss the most

Then some of us are so loyal
That we wear a hat to show
That they do
Have some to spare

Then there are those
Who just don't care and let the rest
Of us witness the mess
That you call my "Wonderful Hair!"

HOPE HAS NO PLACE: HAUNTING MEMORIES TRAPPED BY BARS

I woke one morning
To the sound of happy feet
Going pitter-patter

The sound of *shhhhhh* was followed by the words
"It don't matter,"
Setting off the
Giggles of joyful laughter
From my offsprings
It's this thought that still rings
Through my fleeting heart

For I have awaken to a place that has no trace
Of the land where I wish I could be
The sounds I now hear
Are no longer the things
I hope for

Loud is the clack, when the door cracks
Leaving me with the haunting memory
Of those pitter-patter feet

Though there has been fourteen years of space
My hope is in grace
For there is no other redeeming place
I step out of bed in faith
Knowing that another day of hope has taken yesterday's place

My mind must quickly adjust
From this wanderlust
For you can be sure
In this guarded fortress
There is no mercy to be had

For kindness is mistaken as weakness
I struggle to focus from the bleakness
Realizing no one knows the time or hour
Life is short to those who are obsessed
With ghostly thoughts

For it's the hope I once bought
With the reminiscing thought
Which begins to rot
Gnawing at my plea of innocence
Why does this hope have a position?
In this condemned and final resting place

It's a gritty struggle to maintain my sanity
When I brush my teeth
As the reflection of the man in the mirror
Continues to repeat
Overwhelming my remaining existence
Which is spent
Wondering how I can hope
When I was sentenced
To more time than I could exist

Yet I have a hope that does not live
In this decaying world
It lives in the Kingdom to Come
Decided by the battle
That lies within this man's heart

It's where I've chosen to stand
This waking moment
Because He woke the hope within me
Before the iron shackles took me
From the joyful giggles of the happy feet
When He extended his arms
And showed me how much love could hope for
With a nail in both His hands and feet

ON A JOURNEY OF WHAT F.R.E.E.D.O.M MEANS

Freedom, what is *Freedom*?
Freedom from these *fences*?
The Freedom to *laugh*, *cry* & be *sad*
Or slap Yo head off!
When you disrespect me!

These are some Freedoms
I ponder
When life behind these Bars
Takes a toll on this mind

Because **FREEDOM** is a journey
That spells out
Fleeting, **R**oads, **E**nd,
Except, **D**own, **O**ur **M**inds

This kind of Freedom
Can *build*
Or *tear* down
A man's soul

Therefore, Preparation is crucial.
So lock it down
When unhealthy
Trash talk'n comes around

Protect your mind
At all times
Cause that is
Where the true
Heart of Freedom lives

Complex thinking
Isn't doing all you can
To be set Free

Freedom is
From the tyranny
Of echoed thoughts
Projected by Haunted memories
When the darkness of night
Replaces
The restful safety of light.

Freedom is valuable
Which encourages rebellion
When you try
To force one's hand

It always has the constant
Command of a price,
That warns you
Pursuing selfish freedom
Requires Collateral Damage

The concept of
This kind of Freedom
Has afforded me
To *receive* or *give*
Unmerited favor

It was the Freedom
Of bad Behavior
That created bad Habits
The trails I harmfully blazed
Weren't upon the legacy
I intended to build

Since I realize
The deeds of freedom
I finally recognize
The Awful Monuments
I have founded
In the past

This Freedom I speak of
Has no expiration date.
The strength of this mortar
Lies deep within
The recesses
Of our consciousness

It's the testament
Everyone carries
Through this razor wire
Journey called Freedom.

On this path
No one escapes
The toil
Of being overlooked

Unfortunately, many
Still don't know
What it took

When will you
Wipe the mirror
And take a fresh look
And appreciate that
Freedom is not hindered
By our location

Because the road is covered
With endless mental passages
That comfort us

Like the strength
Of friendship in loyalty
For Joy's greatest companion
Is Freedom, in Christ Jesus,
Until the last breath

So what does Freedom
Mean to you?

Hopefully this journey
Has given you a clue
What it means to you
Before the last breath
Knows you

SHONACH LOKISSON

As a disciple of Loki, I strive to perpetually build and refine my talent with words, both spoken and written. As the world slowly descends into chaos, I relish the moments of peace and serenity when pen meets paper. My writings tend to reflect my faith, and my faith is strengthened by my writing. I am a Heathen in a day and age when we have been forgotten. I stand alone in a crowd and shout to the Gods, "We are here!"

MUSINGS OF A HERETIC

What is Evil? Webster defines evil as "Morally corrupt." Moral is defined as "Conforming to a standard of right behavior; sanctioned by or operative on one's conscience or ethical judgment." So, if evil is to be morally corrupt, and morals are based upon personal conscience and ethics, then the only way a person can be evil is to be judged by someone else's standard. So, essentially, if what you do is different from what I do, and what you say is different from what I say, then you're evil. But no one ever realizes that, because of this, evil is a mirror.

HERESY
A Face of Evil

I have been called evil by more people than I care to admit, but over time that has begged the question, What makes me evil? Is it because I follow the ancient religion of my people? What makes me a heretic, and why does the world perceive that as being evil?

The word "heresy" comes from a Greek word that means choice, or a thing chosen. Yet the modern people look upon heresy as something evil, something to be despised and avoided. The world looks at a heretic as a rebel or a fool, because the meaning of the word has been lost and people have placed their own definition and connotation on the word, neither of which is positive.

But when did making your own choice become something to be condemned? It is my opinion that the reason the world reacts so badly to this is the same reason humans fear the dark. Fear of the unknown.

My name is Shonach Lokisson and I follow the Old Gods of the Norse Pantheon. Because of this, most of the world views me as a heretic, and most only do so because they have been told that that's just what you do in that situation. Any questioning of the set standard will likely end in you getting labeled heretic as well.

In her book *Optimism*, Helen Keller says, "The heresy of one age becomes the orthodoxy of the next." Let's take that quotation and look at when Christianity was new. Was it instantly accepted, or were the men and women who spoke out for this religion beaten and killed as heretics? What was once the most hated faith is now one of the most accepted and revered of all religions. Unfortunately, the inverse is true for Heathens. What was once a well-known and widely accepted faith is now marked as heretical.

Two thousand years ago, I would have been regarded as nothing more than just another Northman, yet in the modern world of acceptable religions, I am called a heretic. I am Asatru, and I ask you, What do you know about the Aesir? Chances are, you know nothing. After all, it is understood that the victors of any conflict dictate history. When my people warred with the Christians in the Viking Age, there was more at stake than land and riches, though my ancestors likely didn't understand that. However, when the Heathens began losing, the Christians began waging a very different war, one that my people weren't prepared for. They didn't know how to retaliate, or even whether they should.

The Christians began to assimilate the Vikings into their society slowly. It started by bribing and baptizing our kings, and after that it snowballed out of control. Today, if you look at the national religion of the Kingdom of Sweden, which was once one of the three Viking kingdoms, you'll see that it is listed as a Protestant country. My people are not gone, but they are few. Why is following in the footsteps of my ancestors evil, but eradicating an entire culture is perfectly acceptable?

Now, I don't say this as an effort to cause dissent. I have brothers who are Christians, and I love them as much as I love my Heathen brothers, so I say this only to bring a simple truth to light.

To those who get labeled as a heretic, I speak to you personally now. The concept of heresy is constantly changing, as Helen Keller stated. If you truly believe in the path that you walk, then don't let anyone influence your decisions. It will be hard to weather the insults and derision, particularly if they come from those you love. I have been there, and I know what it's like to have everyone you care about treat you like an idiot who doesn't know better, or someone who has no shred of decency. I would tell you that it gets better, but that would be a lie. It doesn't get better, but you do get better at dealing with it.

Sometimes the choices we make create a schism between us and our family, and that leads to asking ourselves, "Is it worth it? What's more important, my faith or my family?" Unfortunately, no one can help you with that question. That is something that you have to figure out on your own, but know this: though your choice may mark you as a heretic, you are not alone. Countless others have made the choice before you, and countless others will make it after you. For some of us, making that choice cost us our families, but we find new families that don't judge us for our choices. And regardless of popular opinion, I'm not referring to only people of our chosen religion. I have brothers that don't believe anything similar to me, yet I would trust them with my life.

Why? Because they took the time to get to know me, and didn't just follow the rest of the world's misconceptions.

One of the things that I have lived my life by is the saying, "Blood makes us related, but loyalty makes us family." What makes us so different in the first place? If you compare the many religions, you will find a plethora of similarities, which begs the question, If our faiths, which we view as radically different, can find so much middle ground, why can't we do the same for each other?

The world may know me as a heretic for asking these questions and following this path, and that's fine. Though the world uses the word incorrectly, I understand the original meaning of the word. I was strong enough to make a choice, knowing the cost, and because I did so, I suffered through disputes about my morality, disrespect of my faith, and disregard of my intelligence.

And, yet, when one door closes, another one opens. The things I have lost still haunt me, but the things I have gained give me strength to persevere past the point where I would have given up on my own. So when people look at you with contempt and say, "Heretic!" and name you evil, do not give them a moment's consideration, because the only thing evil in the world is humanity debasing each other for nothing more than personal satisfaction.

Hail the Gods,
Shonach Lokisson

EMERGENCE

So much to do, but so little time . . .

The man came out of the cave, seeing sunlight for the first time in two thousand years. Looking to the sky, he barked a laugh. His fiery red hair blew in the wind, and his sea blue eyes constantly moved, greedily devouring every sight. He stretched forth his hand tentatively, and the familiar weight of his War Spear settled into it. He sighed in relief; it had been so long. A voice spoke from behind him.

"My dear, are you ready?"

The man turned to his wife, smiling as he pulled her close. "Of course I'm ready," he said, confidence in his voice.

Close as she was, she couldn't see the doubt in his eyes. He drew back and looked at her for what he knew would be the last time. She was still beautiful, though centuries of exile were written plainly on her. Her eyes, which had once been so silver as to challenge the brightness of the moon, now gleamed with the furious gray of a rolling storm cloud. Her hair, which was once as shiny black as the midnight sky, was now the deep black of shadows.

"Go," he said, before he lost his nerve, "Flee this place. Time is short, and you need to be far away when it begins." She rested her head against his chest for a moment. Whispering a prayer, she then turned and fled towards the horizon that was quickly fading from sight. As he watched her go, a tear slowly crept down his face. At that moment, a star streaked across the sky, falling from the heavens. It had begun. The man wiped away the tear just as the shadows pulsed. As they settled, a woman materialized.

The man began to speak. "They will be hunting Sigyn. Find her, protect her, and make sure she is alive when this is over." He spoke sharply, inviting no argument.

The woman nodded her head, and light flickered across her face, bringing the monstrous beauty to illumination. The left side of her face was beautiful. Her eye was as green as a sparkling emerald; her skin was the pale white of porcelain; and her hair was the blue-black of raven's wings. The right side of her face, however, was horrendous. Her skin was rotted and peeled back, revealing the skull beneath; her hair was tangled and missing in patches, and her eye socket was filled with an orange light, flickering like a malevolent flame.

"As you command, Father." She bowed, then slowly faded.

The man nodded as more tears rolled down his face. It was almost over. His wife and daughter were safe, and he was free. Almost. He brought his fists in close, clenching them to his chest. He seemed to be struggling for a moment, then his eyes snapped open. They were no longer blue; instead, they glowed a yellow gold color, and they seemed to promise mischief. He thrust his arms out to either side, and armor appeared. It, too, was yellow gold, and was etched with foxes. Stars began falling in quick succession, and in the distance, a wolf howled. The man smiled.

"Hunt, my son. Hunt."

The world around the man fluctuated, then snapped back into focus, but the surroundings had changed. He now stood on a bridge, facing a man wearing bright silver armor and holding a great sword.

At the same time, both men spoke. "Let's begin."

They charged each other, one laughing in amusement, one roaring in anger. As the Fox and the Guardian clashed, the worlds began burning. So much to do, but so little time . . .

DILEMMA A.K.A. STROKEGAMEVICIOUS

Dilemma is the problem that most artists run into when they find out there's someone else just as skilled. My Stroke Game Vicious stems from a couple of things. One includes a pen and paper with my life in metaphors. The other is for the imagination. I am a Dilemma and my stroke game vicious.

A NEW CREATION

> "Therefore if any man be in Christ, he is a new creature: old
> things are passed away; behold, all things are become new."
> 2 Corinthians 5: 17

I was thinking the plan that He's got for me, was truly not for me,
When obviously, it could include a lot of peace,
Honestly that bothered me, because being Christian was comedy,
I knew people that were believers, but that wasn't a part of me,
I thought . . . how could I see? That somebody died for me,
I felt like Thomas at the Resurrection . . . You have to show me
    before I believe,
So I picked up a Bible not really wanting to read what it said,
But when I did read, I didn't have enough knowledge to understand
    what I read,
I got helped but didn't care, because when I prayed I felt like he wasn't
    there.
Not only that, but I saw nonbelievers prospering and I thought
    it wasn't fair,
So what I do? More sinning. Fornication was just the beginning,
See I didn't find Divine intervention until I entered in prison,
But in the meantime, since I've been living I didn't smoke or drink, I
    thought I was doing something right,
Not knowing that fornication and adultery kept me out of
    The Book of Life,
See at first I didn't know that . . . and I ain't trying to go back,
So to stay on the straight and narrow . . . I need a different road map,
Now, let me reintroduce myself, see I'm a Child of God,
I've been down the block of sin but my God works around the clock,
I don't know if you can count or not, it don't matter, as long as you
    know, who you can count on to provide food for that counter top,
The devil's around a lot and he's not down to stop tempting you but
    luckily Jesus always surrounds His flock,
When my vision's dark, the devil's made his mark but him beating my
    God is like me trying to drown a shark,
Now is that logical? I know it's kind of comical because a shark has
    gills, so that makes it impossible,
But that's only for man, God's Power astronomical, so what we can't
    do, for Him it's not an obstacle,
See The Lord's my major source of income,
He provides me with the things that I need on top of that
    and then some,

So the same thing He did for me He can do for you, that's
    if you choose,
He'll stick by your side without any use of super glue, Jesus
    is super cool,
No matter the color of your skin, we all turn to Him for one goal like a
    Rubik's Cube,
Now before you clap I don't want to take full credit as the author,
Because while you're thanking me I'm thanking my FATHER.

EXPECTATIONS?

I feel I'm required to not be rejected,
Because I tend to express what you expected,
Nothing but the best but . . .
What if I don't meet those expectations?
Would my name be tainted?
Would you second guess your favorite?
Or would you express some hatred because of the lack
of excess language,
All because time and time again I prove to be a wordsmith, now you
decide where the standard is aimed, I'm Hannibal . . .
Because I feed off my brothers like I'm cannibal raised,
I mean what you expect? It's simple . . . for me not to be simple,
Always Direct like Cox Cable has dwindled,
See? Another unnecessary word . . . Why couldn't I have just said "fell
off" or "waste of time"?
I gotta make things difficult that's the expectation because of how I
trained my mind,
To take a line and make it mine then make it rhyme,
And take it one step further to blow it out of proportion like I'm
making mines,
The name Dilemma but the problem is the ones that believe in me . . .
Be leaving me but like it or not,
That's a lot of weight on my shoulders . . . and I ain't doing squat,
So don't depend on me or depend on the pen because when I fail you
that label will get pinned on me,
A big disappointment . . . because a critic decides to criticize,
Yet if I'm not doing good don't let my downfalls be minimized,
I'm human just like you . . . I may say things different and
metaphorically format sentences,
But that's because to get that cheese I take my Kraft more serious,
I'm not in here to just sit and fill a chair,
If I feel inspired . . . humidifier . . . I'll get up and clear the air,
So don't hold me to a higher Standard,
I don't hold a key to help you get in any doors . . . I'm not a lanyard,
So expect nothing less of me than to give you the best of me
of what's projected,
Just know I don't neglect what you expect but be willing to expect
the unexpected,

FIGURES . . .

I'm trying to be a better father figure,
Since I figured my father didn't want to bother with us,
Was tired of living back and forth without a pot to piss in,
I got so used to moving I can't say it's not addictive,
It never was a thought that I would mimic,
The same footsteps once I looked back . . . shoot my father did it,
Still have no idea who he is though my pops was missin',
I made every effort to not be in my pop's position,
I felt just like my father . . . figures,
I didn't see this coming . . . I feel like I lost the vision,
But am I the victim?
Naw . . . and time is ticking,
And change was supposed to start with me but I reside in prison,
But now my mind has shifted,
I'm thinking outside of the box this time instead of climbing in it,
I'll defy the limit and expectations the system said that I couldn't finish,
I'm not a number and I'm not gone succumb to the opposition,
Of me being a person because of a cop's intentions,
I'm not gonna listen nor make any propositions with no politicians,
So they can take their loud malicious gossip with em',
I've suffered enough consequences,
But how do we get even when the odds against us?
Common sense would say stop pretending,
Like everything is ok when this box we live in,
Is so infected by greed we need amoxicillin,
It's funny how violence is not offensive,
It's become the norm like washing dishes or prisons
    with locks & fences,
Hands up don't shoot that's what was brought to millions,
Yet we still can't stop the killin',
Whether it's now or back then there's not a difference,
From being shot by a cop or lynching,
This the generation my kids growing up in and it's not appealin',
No need to block the feelin',
Because they so used to it that it doesn't shock the children,
Crazy isn't it?
Figures . . .

PUSHING "SUE" ASIDE

Though it's nothing nice,
The thought crossed her mind once or twice,
And she got the right to know,
Why she's become quite the joke and continuously viewed
    under a microscope,
Self-esteem low because she's too ugly to be good enough,
Or because she's way too cute and don't look as tough,
    the shit's wrong,
She might as well be in the same category as acne . . . cause she's
    constantly being picked on,
A lot of people being relentless and she gets tired of being defensive,
So to fit in wit bitches she sent provocative pictures,
And now they copy and send'em to friends who shocked
    when they witness,
That she's let herself be the victim of the world and now she resent it,
So once again she take a slice on her wrist because it's a risk she's
    willing to take,
What's astounding is the hate that surrounds her and she feels
    she'll break,
But she's tired of being laughed at . . . her comments getting backlash,
So she deactivates her Facebook and gets rid of her Snapchat,
When she's alone is when she thinks about it cause it's her way out,
She's thinking, stay out my head . . . I got a family that loves me,
Sometimes she asks God why he made her so ugly,
She feels if you loved me . . . you wouldn't put me in this predicament,
Knowing words hurt . . . and you knew I'd be sensitive,
Someone showed her the ropes but she'll make hers better,
So follow Sue on Twitter . . . that's if you want to hang together . . .

        Sincerely,
        Sue

LUKE ANTHEM SINCLAIR

*My writing is like my life—All over the place. I have poetry and prose,
fiction and non. Although I might look like the quintessential suburban
white dude, my life and experiences are more akin to the multiracial
cacophony of the western hemisphere; only the trailer park, hood,
barrio version. I write about what moves me: love, faith, and Kaizen
(continuous improvement). I am passionate about justice reform and
connections with people. I hope my writing makes you cry, smile, and
think deeply. You will see unrealized love and political statements. There
will be extraordinary life experiences mixed with nonfictional characters
as well as poetic descriptions of divine works. Finally, a word of caution.
Read slowly: too much of me too quickly could blow your mind.*

FIRST GLANCE OF SKY

I took my first glance of sky.
Crystal to ice blue as I took my first
Gaze through the window.

The window: streaked dirty pane crossed by
1, 2, 3, 4, 5, bars parallel created to be my
Impenetrable portal to the heavens.

I can see the wind!

Slowly beckoning and pulling the magnificent
Marshmallow clouds in an oh-so-slow
Race across my gaze.

Freedom!

No concrete, numbers, or bars. No keys with screaming faces.
Just the endless endless expanse of pasture for the
Ever billowing buffalo clouds.

Freedom.

One day I'll be a cloud, and I'll move with
Obese slowness across someone else's gaze.

But today,
I took my first glance of sky.

UNIVERSAL WORSHIP

God spoke, Life in His words. We'll call it transitive verbs.
Because that action's absurd
To those cursed to think the earth first began with a burst,
Ha! Or really a Bang.
Naw
This ain't no accidental reign.
No, my God is sovereign
The answer to every problem
The whole universe sings to Him
Super sonic !
Super . . . sonic
Over . . . sound.
The stars exist on a certain frequency
The dust of the earth, yo Even that speaks to me.
'Cause it is me and 'cause He breathed
I will sing frequently.
Freely joining easily the grass, flower, tree, tumbleweed symphony.
And I will praise all my days when I think how you razed
Adam up from the dust yeah, I'm so amazed.
Every molecule, every follicle
Is a reflecting pool shining back your glorious face.
The lion roars, "Yahweh!" The eagle soars, "Yahweh!"
Even the prey sings praise in his jaws.
The trees clap their hands, the shifting sand it understands
The ocean worships you, yeah the ground applauds.
I lift my eyes to the skies and this beautiful night
Is painted so perfect my soul ignites.
So I'm going to buzz with the bees and I'm going breeze with the air.
Watch the wind whip the mountain tops,
Altitude player.
Yeah, He plays the mountains go get His album.
I will cop it like His mercy how it's new every morning
And I will rock it till my eyes close and people mourn me . . .
Just don't mourn me.
'Cause now I'll dance with the clouds
And I will worship Him loud
Until the rain wets my face and my hair!
And I will praise Him like David
Till I'm dancin' buck naked,
I don't care, I won't care!
Jesus is the reason that all creation is breathin' hymns of praise let us
    meet in the air.

35

Singing "Holy, Holy, Holy You are Worthy!"
Let your Hallelujah shoot like a flare!
Say Hallelujah. Ya
Say Hallelujah. Ya
With all creation sing, "Holy God, Holy~ ~God."

I DON'T WANT TO SEE YOU!

Every time I see you my heart skips . . . butterflies dance . . . my brain
    goes on vacation.
I'm talkin' about for you, I lose it!
That's my initial reaction but then the pain sets in.

A fleeting glance.

A glimpse and gone.

A few spoke words of greeting but no depth; surface with
    no connection.
I don't want to know you like that. I don't want to hear about your life
    without me in it.

I want you to expose yourself to me!
I want to laugh and cry . . . together.
I want to experience you, and you me, like two futuristic explorers
    delving into the uncharted territory of each other.
The infinitive reaches of boundless love!

But that's not possible is it?
Not now . . .

Therefore I don't want to know you.

I don't want to see you.

Because in the not knowing . . . the not seeing . . . the pain may
    diminish. My heart will begin to forget,
And I can tell myself it was just a dream . . .
Not real but fantasy.

It would be a lie.

But the lie won't hurt as bad as seeing and never knowing you. Talking,
    but never really experiencing you.
So go!
Don't turn back!

Live your life!

And if we ever meet again, maybe then we'll make it work.
But right now it's just too much hurt. That's why . . .

I don't want to see you!

UNTITLED

This is to those whom I have hurt. To the people whose lives have been all but destroyed by my choices and actions. I pray that you can rise from the ashes.

No one can imagine the pain that you still feel all these years later. You were not even there that night; that cold October night when I took the life of your father, husband, brother and uncle. He was an honored war veteran, a loving husband and father, and I with no rhyme or reason took his life from him. The incident lasted no more than a few seconds, and almost 2 decades later I still don't know how many people have suffered because of that split second decision.

You need to know that there was no provocation. He was nothing but friendly to me. We were bullies and I was the worst one; the instigator . . . the perpetrator. No words can express my remorse. Nothing I can say will ever "make it better." If I were to solve world hunger or end human trafficking it would not justify my actions that night. I am not attempting to mitigate or lessen what I did. That would be to lessen who he was and belittle the life he led. My goal, at this point, is to magnify his life. To let his spirit live on and touch people still today. My mission is to let his life and his death impact young people to make better choices than I made.

I have not mentioned his name out of reverence and respect for you and your privacy. But I hope you see this and know that it is you to whom I am speaking. I hope you see my heart.

And to those of you who don't know me or of what I am speaking, my admonition is to love. Cherish life as the gift it is, and smother young people with love. Even the teenage boy who may be a little bit awkward. Because you never know, your love and encouragement may be just what he needs to not end up like me.

Respectfully, Inmate X

LIVING VS. BEING ALIVE

To be Alive is to thrive! The spark of life is audacious. This is the thrilling existence of a person submerged in purpose.

Living is going through the motions. Almost meaningless. It is a thread of life, barely existent, wallowing in purposelessness.

Alive is emotion- Hi/low rollercoaster on the edge of one's seat.

Living is drear- Hollow, being swept along with the passing winds.

When God breathed into Adam's nostrils, Adam became a living soul ... he existed. But when Eve came onto the scene Adam came Alive; they named the animals and ruled the garden.

Are you Alive or just Living?

John Eldridge, in his book *Wild at Heart*, says, "Don't ask yourself what the world needs. Ask yourself what makes you come alive. Because what the world needs is Men and Women who have come Alive."

ELZIE HOOKS, JR.

As a meditationist, my works on loneliness and the imagination highlight the power of feeling alone and the sorrow of what should have been.

LIFE'S EQUAL OPPORTUNITY DESTROYER

Loneliness is an experience that affects humans equally, it is an invisible predator that is watchful and stealthy. We are encountered by this force at a point of weakness. I met this individual while strolling across the prison facility one day. She just appeared next to me without physical form, but I could sense and feel a presence that was friendly and comfortable. It would become clear later that this was a clever disguise, because my future was in jeopardy of being lost.

As we continued on our way, I asked the stranger, "What is your name"? The reply with a sultry voice was, "Loneliness." So, I asked her with a curious voice, "Where did you come from?" She said softly, "You summoned me." I then asked, being confused and suspicious, "When and how?" She answered sternly, "You don't remember." "No, I don't" was my answer. Loneliness then said calmly, "The moment you began dwelling on your past failures and their consequences, you got my attention. As you continued doing that, a door in my dimension was open so that I could enter your dimension. And that's how I showed up out of nowhere!" "I see," was my reply.

"But what are your intentions?" was my next question. I could sense Loneliness had moved in closer to me, to a whisper-like distance, then she said sympathetically, "I know you miss the family laughter during holiday meals and at special celebrations. I know you wanted to stand with the family when the newest members of the clan entered the world and when a loved one left it. I know that you deeply regret not being a part of the growing up years of your children's lives and that you long to experience love with a woman that transcends the physical."

My response with an agitated voice was, "What do you want with me?" Loneliness moved to face me, as if in a confrontational posture. With unflinching words she said, "I came to destroy your future with despair!" Her demeanor changed and now the true intent of her heart was clearly evident. I responded angrily with, "So, you are going to kill my future with despair." The retort with a curt voice was, "Yes, if you are going to focus on the past, then there's no need for the future."

I was then grabbed by tentacle like arms that had strong suction cups which encased hypodermic needles. She begin injecting an overdose of despair into me. I could not free myself from the arms of Loneliness and like cyanide gas the lethal effects of despair were squeezing the breath of life from my soul. Somehow I made it to the cell and fell to my knees in desperation. I cried out to the Divine for help! I said, "Please release me from the deadly clutches of Loneliness." He answered with, "Trust in me and your future will be far brighter than your darkest past."

It was then that the death embrace of Loneliness was broken and exchanged for the loving embrace of peace and hope for a better tomorrow.

IMAGINE THIS

I was feeling the ill effects of my wife's pregnancy. The unorthodox appetite, the unfamiliar tiredness, the unnatural desire of sleeping a lot and the breaking out of teeny-weeny bumps on my thighs. This kid was driving me bananas and it was not born yet. Of course, I played a role in all this so it was fitting that I share some of the experience. However, I could not help but think, "What have you gotten yourself into and is this stuff an ominous sign of things to come?" Perhaps this is why parents today say that they are pregnant. I struggle with the idea of a man referring to himself as being pregnant but this experience has taught me what they mean. At any rate, I was looking forward to holding our son and that would soon be a reality.

"Elzie, let's to go to the hospital." I asked, "What's going on?" My wife's response was, "What do you think is going on, my water has broken." So, off to the hospital we went. Once there she was quickly admitted and taken to a room. She was resting on the bed when the contractions really started, it spooked me at first because it was clear that there was some discomfort involved. I could tell this because of the slight groaning, her uneven movement and the light sweat that was beginning to slide down the side of her face. The nurse came into the room and asked, "Darling, how close are the contractions." Her response in between groans and squeezing the blood out of my hand was, "really close." "Okay let me see how far you have dilated." After checking, the nurse said, "You are ready to deliver the baby, let me get the doctor." The nurse asked my wife, "Do you want a shot for pain?" She said, "Yes."

I knew the time was now at hand when three nurses and a doctor quietly hustled into my wife's hospital room. I was standing on the right side of her bed still holding her hand as they transformed the bed area into a delivery station. The doctor was really calm and smiled at me as he walked up to the bed. The nurse handed him a needle as he told the soon to be mother, "We going to give you something that will help with the pain." At that point he asked her to roll over on her side where he inserted the needle into the lower back area that was really close to the spine. After the injection, I helped her return to the original position and the doctor said, "Let's deliver this baby boy."

I heard of fathers who passed out because they could not handle the birthing process. But my intent was to see this miracle of God exit his original home and enter ours. As two nurses took positions on both sides of the bed, the other nurse stood just left of the doctor. The doctor was sitting on a small four-legged chrome stool, it had a round black leather seat with four small black wheels at the base of each leg which provided him mobility in the working area.

No one said anything to me, so I took my position behind the doctor peering over his right shoulder—just like a baseball umpire that's crouched behind the back-catcher waiting to call balls and strikes. However, I was awaiting the arrival of our son.

Alas, it was show time! I begin to look at the portal of life as our son was entering the world. The doctor told my wife to give a good push, and this went on several times. After traveling the short distance from inner darkness to outer light, he was received by the doctor who passed him to the nurse who was standing on his left side. She walked softly to a designated area and proceeded to clean the baby up. His short limbs extended outwardly while the tiny digits at the ends of his hands and feet were flickering like flames on a fire. The nurse wrapped him up and with a warm smile gave him to me. Although I had held precious treasures before, this one was mine. You see my grandmother ran a day care business and had long since taught me how to hold young babies. So, our baby's uneven movement and occasional stretching were uneasy to manage at first, but adjustments were made and he stayed in my arms. A couple of days later we went home.

As time passed he grew from infant to childhood to teenager and to adulthood. I remember celebrating his first birthdays, they were exciting times as everyone stood around him laughing and talking. Of course he didn't understand what the hoopla was all about, but who cared. I remember playing with him while sitting on the living room floor and out of nowhere he took his first steps without my assistance—sweet!

I remember helping him with his school work and watching him go through the experience of winning and losing a first love. I remember watching him excel in sports and teaching him how to drive my car. I remember standing next to him as he was entering matrimony with his life partner.

As you can tell, I am a proud parent and like all proud parents nostalgia occasionally grips our heart. We look back when this happens to re-experience simpler times with our children; times that were full of meaningful and significant events that made life worth living because we had someone to live for. However, for me nostalgia is very different and that's because the experiences I witnessed were only in my imagination.

SHANNON D. HUNT A.K.A. SHANNON THE APPREHENSIVE

A life of foster care, juvenile detention centers, and level E facilities has only shaped me for a life of incarceration. The battle is not prison; the battle is the transition from secular to holy. The compilation before you is of struggle and pain and, of course, the ultimate change of mind and will. What was once a hopeless act of survival by way of criminal inventions has now become a hopeful pursuit of the Godly, by way of self denial. As a poet/songwriter and musician, I try to articulate in many ways the struggle of prison life, as well as what it means to be a Christian behind the fence. I express my anger, my explicit thoughts, as well as my praise and frustration . . .

(IS My Momentum)

HOW I FEEL?

My style is too unique. I hope you haters aren't offended,
Vice-grip lifestyle, so I'm jus trying to keep the tension.
Couldn't do it on my own I keep a selfish ambition.
Pride comes before a fall, I'm just tryna keep from tripping.
I never knew happiness and joy keep escaping me.
Depression isn't pretty, but she the only one who fading me.
I understand in these chains I'm the only one who caging me.
Been falling for so long, I'm doubting if Jesus even saving me.
Love is a stranger because we were never acquainted.
Me and hate are familiar because she was the parent that raised us.
Hearing the same thang from family, who swear they love me.
Get my hopes up on Saturday just to fall on Sunday.
So sick of men saying that they feel my pain.
A heavy dose of kiss my ass in this syringe, trying to kill these veins.
I have dynamite for emotions so don't spark that flame.
But nobody wants to take you seriously until they hear that bang.
How I feel? If it wasn't for Jesus I'd probably end my life.
I've been through hell from the beginning with no end in sight.
I try to make the right turns, but they never turn out right.
And just when I think the fear of darkness is gone, they
      turn out the lights.

That's how I feel.

(I—M Momentum)

PIECE OF PAPER

This piece of paper is where I begin my thoughts and end my conclusions.

This piece of paper does not judge or criticize, but it does motivate.

This piece of paper is still a piece of paper. The only difference is that it's tattooed with my secrets. Secrets such as I wish the whole world explode into a million pieces because mankind is corrupt and evil, plus, I long for death. I wish I could plant a bomb on the car of every politician, and be an eyewitness to each detonation. Lawmakers and lobbyists I would like to personally disembowel because their regards of the people are zero, their intentions are those of personal gain.

You see this piece of paper understands me, and even if it doesn't it sure as hell has a way of making it seem as if it did, which is more than I can say about most people.

This piece of paper is still a piece of paper. The only difference is that it knows my fears. Fears such as no matter how good it gets, it's only a matter of time before that good turns ugly, because that's the story of my life. Love is the ultimate fear. Those who are supposed to love me, I care less for as each day passes.

This piece of paper, I don't need to love me, only to hear as I vent.

This piece of paper assists me in coping with life.

This piece of paper is still a piece of paper, the only difference is that it knows my pain. Pain such as me being abandoned and left to rot in DHS, being mistreated in foster homes, abused and emotionally neglected, rejected by society.

This piece of paper is where I begin my thoughts and end my conclusions.

This piece of paper is still a piece of paper. The only difference is that it's about me and not you.

(I—M Momentum)

HYPOCRITE

1   Out the gate, let me state this: you're a sorry excuse for a Christian. This conclusion which I have reached is based on careful observation of the way you've been living.

2   You're the biggest hypocrite I know, telling ppl that Jesus heals while you're sicker than most. Tryna put a smile on . . . hoping to convince others that your faith is a mile long.

3   But I know you, dude, you're weak & you're brittle—"handle with care" should be your label because you're a fragile individual.

4   So you can't fool me with your bible in hand, the same hand that was just peddling vials & grams. The hand that shed blood for gain, that gained you life in the pen. Eventually they'll see you for who you really are . . . the same person you've always been.

5   You were a failure then, and you're a failure now, you'll neva get it together; you're a joke, a rebellious clown, and every time you fall, it's at that time that you realize that you're in this world alone, because the Christians who are supposed to lift you up are the same ones hurling stones.

6   You ain't figured it out yet? Friends ain't friends, and ya family ain't shit. Death comes sweet because life is a bitch. So pray all you want, but you're the same lump of clay, and there's a lot of broken pottery, dog, but you're the only one on display.

7   In fact, I'm sick of lookin' at you bro, have been for the past 28 years. Do us both a favor and don't bring yo ass back to this mirror.

8   Finish hiding in your emotions because solitary seems perfect. Fall back and if they notice, your excuse is the church did it. Self reflection will get you low, so burn some purp with it—isolation on its peak, that's highly conservative.

9   And while ya at it, throw away everything you worked for like that ain't pertinent—like God don't do miracles no matter what you learned or heard of it.

10 And since God's the driver, he might have went over the curb a bit and if you don't care what people think, then why are you digesting a 3rd of it?

11 Damn, I'm sick of being you. But, what I can't understand is how on earth you proud to be me. That's like the felon who just got life, but is already proud to be free.

12 When he should be broken at best, that slogan hits close to the chest, but when you focused, no matter what I throw at you, you quoting that you chosen and blest.

13 But I gotta give it to you, because you do this one thing right, which isn't bad advice for my peers—and that's this: life is a course and from start to finish line should all be done at this mirror.

(I—M Momentum)

VIGOROUS VERSATILITY

1 I USED TO SEE THE DEVIL IN MY DREAMS WHEN I WAS A KID, AND HIS DEMONS USED TO LAUGH AT ME EVERY TIME I MADE MISTAKES. I USED TO LASH OUT AT SCHOOL AND THE TEACHERS DIDN'T UNDERSTAND THE PROGRESSIVE AGGRESSION BEING PROJECTED FROM A KID THAT WAS BEING RAISED BY THE STATE.

2 I USED TO CRY AND ROCK MYSELF TO SLEEP AT NIGHT, WITH MY HEADPHONES ON, LISTENING TO MARY J. BLIGE, MONICA, AND JODECI, I WAS ALONE IN LIFE, SO I ACTED AN ASS AND DIDN'T CARE WHAT ANYBODY THOUGHT. I JUST WANTED SOMEBODY TO NOTICE ME.

3 I WANTED TO GET AHEAD IN LIFE, FAR FROM POOR, BUT NOT QUITE A SPOONFED LIFE, SURELY NOT A BEGGIN' LIFE. I WANTED TO LEAVE A LEGACY BEFORE I DIED, AND WHEN I DO HOPEFULLY I'LL SEE WHAT HEAVEN'S LIKE.

4 I NEVER HAD A CHILDHOOD. I WENT FROM THE CRADLE TO THE STREETS, BUT THAT'S NORMAL IN MY HOOD, SO I GUESS I WAS COOL WITH IT. I TRIED TO COMMIT SUICIDE BY HANGING MYSELF FROM A LIGHT FIXTURE, BUT I GUESS I WAS TOO MUCH OF A COWARD TO FOLLOW THROUGH WITH IT.

5 PEOPLE TELL ME THAT I WEAR MY HEART ON MY SLEEVE SOMETIME, BUT THE OLD ME WAS HEARTLESS AND I'M A NEW CREATION, SO A BARRIER OR A WALL IS PROBABLY WHAT I NEED SOMETIMES.

6 BECAUSE WHEN I LOVE IT'S DEEP, AND I HATE TO LOVE A FAKE PERSON. BUT SOMETIMES YOU JUST CAN'T HELP YOURSELF BECAUSE YOU DON'T FIND OUT TILL THINGS GET REAL THAT THAT INDIVIDUAL IS WORTHLESS.

7 THEY SAY THE STREETS BREED CRIMINALS; WELL, I SAY POLITICS DO, TOO. MOST POLITICIANS ARE CORRUPT AND IT'S BECAUSE OF THEIR DECISIONS THAT PEOPLE PICK UP DRUGS AND KICK DOORS, ALL SO THEIR KIDS WILL HAVE SOME FOOD.

8 I'D RATHER DIE ON MY FEET THEN TO LIVE ON MY KNEES, BUT I SEE NOTHING WRONG WITH TAKING A HANDOUT AND IF YOUR MISSION IN LIFE IS TO CONTINUE BEING A STATISTIC, THEN YOU FALL INTO MY DEFINITION OF WHAT I CALL A SELL OUT.

9   A MAN IS NO BETTER THAN THE COMPANY HE KEEPS, AND HE WHO WALKS WITH THE WISE MEN WILL HIMSELF BE WISE. AND WE KNOW FROM WHAT WE SOW THAT WE WILL REAP, AND HE WHO WALKS WITH THE FOOLISH WILL HIMSELF BE DESPISED.

10   AND ME, I'M JUST AN ORDINARY MAN WITH AN EXTRAORDINARY VISION, AN APPREHENSIVE INDIVIDUAL. AND, IN MY MOMENTS OF SIMPLICITY, I TEND TO SPEAK EXPLICITLY, SELF-CONSECRATED I CONVEY THE TRUTH WHEN IT'S CRITICAL.

11   LOQUACIOUS, VOCIFEROUS, NO FAKENESS, I'M JUST DIFFERENT. I'M PATIENT, LOW MAINTENANCE, FULL OF LIFE AND I'M VIGOROUS. MY LOYALTY HAS NO END, THAT'S WHY I KEEP FAMILY, FUCK FRIENDS, AND EXCUSE MY SPEECH BUT WHEN YOUR BACK IS TURNED IT'LL BE YOUR HOMIES THAT PUT THE KNIFE IN.

12   ETHICS OVER CONVENIENCE, TRUTH OVER POPULARITY. I STAY THE SAME; I'LL NEVER SELL OUT OR BE BOUGHT, AND LIKE A PRECIOUS GEM, I'D NEED A GOOD DIAMOND CUTTER JUST TO CRYSTALIZE MY THOUGHTS.

13   WHEN I WAS A KID, I GANG BANGED AND SOLD DRUGS, BUT THAT WAS THEN. I'M 28 YEARS OLD NOW. I'M HONEST AND HOLD A JOB AND A GOOD REPUTATION WHILE I'M IN PRISON. WHY? BECAUSE I'M GROWN NOW.

14   SO, POUR OUT A LITTLE LIQUOR FOR THE DEAD HOMIES, BUT THIS SHIT IS GETTING OLD. I SWEAR, IT'S GETTING OLD.

15   PUTTING IN WORK FOR THE DEAD HOMIES, THE SHIT IS GETTING OLD, I SWEAR, IT'S GETTING OLD.

16   ANOTHER FUNERAL FOR A DEAD HOMIE, IT'S GETTING OLD, I SWEAR, IT'S GETTING OLD.

17   NOBODY WANTS TO BE ANOTHER DEAD HOMIE, WHY? THE SHIT IS OLD, I SWEAR IT GOT OLD.

(I—M Momentum)

MORYÉ D. CHANDLER, SR. A.K.A. BUSINESS END
A.K.A. SHOF'TIM

My name is Moryé D. Chandler, Sr. Writing—for me—is an art form and, as I've experienced, serves as a means of relief from life's challenges.

The styles of writing most suited to me are prose and, occasionally, poetry—especially socially conscious submissions. I hope to reach the reader where they are, just as other writers have reached me.

I am 45 years old and the father of three gifted sons and one extremely brilliant daughter. They spur my desire to succeed.

. . . THIS IS NOT A SONG . . .

Freedom is a religion
Freedom is what you make it
Freedom: is when your government is ready to take it.

Freedom is greedy pockets
Freedom goin' to war
Freedom hoggin' the money while you keepin' me poor

Freedom to be a beggar
Freedom to stand tall
Freedom is recognizing freedom ain't freedom at all

Freedom express love
Freedom is such a lock
Freedom for me is subject to your multiple shots

Freedom is Donald Trump
Freedom is Giuliani
Freedom is when a hollow point invading ya body

Freedom to wear a badge
Freedom to pack a gun
Freedom to kill a 12 year old . . . somebody's son

Freedom is Flint, Michigan
Yep! It's like that
Freedom is dirty water flowin' outta tha tap

Freedom is reparations
Freedom is my seed
Freedom is 40 acres so I grow what I need

Freedom is underfunding
Education and schools
Freedom is makin' us look like some goddamn fools

Freedom, if you a Haitian
Freedom, you outta luck
Freedom is when they see your pain and they don't give a fuck

Freedom is politicians
Freely callin' me "Thug"
Freedom is blamin' me when it's your kid on drugs

Freedom is shootin' dope
Freedom is all night
Freedom: An epidemic when the user is white

I say: freedom is shootin' dope
Freedom is all night
Freedom: An epidemic when the user is white

Freedom is FaceBook
Freedom is now live
Freedom is makin' money offa somebody life

Freedom is pointin' fingers
Freedom is tellin' lies
Freedom to cover up but ca-ma-ras don't lie

Freedom is buildin' prisons
Freedom fillin' 'em up
Freedom is dirty money when you gettin' a cut

Freedom was never equal
Freedom is Jim Crow
Freedom is never justice when it's just who you know

Freedom is executions
Freedom is done wrong
Freedom is when he dead he innocent after all

Freedom is how I breathe
Freedom to protest
Freedom is when my kid wear a bulletproof vest

Freedom is Business End
Freedom is who I am
Imprisonment took the body but you'll never take the man

   . . . THIS IS NOT A SONG . . ..

THE TREE AND ME

I have seen many things over the years of this experience—prison I mean. I can still vividly recall that cold, December night as I rode on that cramped, white van so full of dark-skinned humans. To some, the ride was as commonplace as the drawing of the next breath, to others, like myself—well, I could have been preparing for a trip to the surface of the moon; surely the perils facing such a journey would be less daunting than those before me at the time. For myself and a few others, this was a most uncommon sensation; after all, we were chained hand and foot, en route to a prison camp, an interment of sorts. It was cold and mildly damp despite the bodies stacked in that vehicle. I recall looking out the window as—with each passing mile— my freedom slipped further into the annals of history; I suppose it was therefore befitting that ice had begun to form on the inside of these orifices which permitted one to witness the distortion of their own future. For the profound abundance of life present in this cramped conveyance, coldness and death seemed tangible, seemed—in fact—to proliferate . . . my life was over.

Fast forward eight years . . .

One evening, after I had arrived at my current location, I came across a tree. *"A tree?!"* you ask? Well, don't be quick to presumptions; I know a man I find highly intelligent who once entered into profound discourse with a tree. After my many experiences—moving within this system—it had been some time since I'd seen, let alone touched a tree; and now here I am.

I remember the season with a certain familiarity; it was autumn and the leaves were still falling from this tree. You know the time of year where the evening air is sort of cool and damp, filled with the smell of downed foliage. I was so happy to finally be around something natural—sturdy as this tree was. I looked forward, past the coming winter with its mind-numbing dreariness, and on to the spring where this living thing would return again to life! Cloudy, depressing days seemed to just barely creep by. The brutality of icy northern gales carried watery mist which seemed to search out any surface on which to cling; still, the tree stood firm. Days turned into weeks, those again into months until finally it arrived. I saw them: "Look there! The limbs of this wonderful tree were starting to stir!" No, the brutal winter had not vanquished the tree. My excitement grew . . . just like those tiny buds. "Hello tree, good spring awakening! I have been patiently waiting on you," said I to the tree. As the days passed and the buds grew, so consumed by this tree was I that the days appeared to run one in to the other; my excitement had taken over. What would the buds in turn produce? Would they blossom into some great aromatic orchestra? Oh how I waited on that tree!

I remember waking early one spring morning, excited to witness more of this tree's awakening when some horrible thing assailed upon me. "Ewww, what in the world is that stench?! Who pissed all over the outdoors?!" Quick disclaimer: I don't personally subscribe to this rumor, but . . . I'd heard that aircraft emptied their human waste at high altitude, but my goodness, had some of this made its way onto my courtyard having been carried aloft on the winds? So thrown off by the odor, I contradicted my own logic by taking repeated breaths of this foulness in hopes of discovering its source. "Sniff, Sniff! Sniff . . . Sniiiff." To my total surprise, or better said, my dismay, my disgust, it was the tree! Oh tree, seat of my enthusiasm; how I waited on you, held out hope, waited and waited and waited—in full anticipation . . . on this. My lovely tree, what is this stench? What wretched odor forthwith have you belched? My mind was whirling with query. This tree had blossomed so beautifully, a canopy of white so high and pristine that the clouds above must have envied its hue. While those clouds may have envied, I was beyond glad that they were there—a vaporous barrier between the life-giving warmth of the sun's rays and this sturdy, awakened from its slumber, beautifully crowned, stinky, smelly, old tree.

Someone must by now surely wonder; *"Why is he going on and on about this tree?"* Well, I'll tell you. This tree, the very one that betrayed my olfactories . . . changed; it transformed. As the spring blew in and the white blossoms were carried aloft, in their place were new, tender leaves. As I watched this tree go through its rejuvenation, I began to look back at myself; in my life I took inventory; "Am I transforming?"

I believed I have been "awakened," enlightened as it were, and surely someone, several someone's in fact, have—in times past—looked at me, have seen the wretched likeness of my nature and have loathed the foulness of my presence. And so still I look at that tree. I watched it grow, I witnessed this tree provide a place of rest for the birds of the air, I looked on as this tree offered itself as a sanctuary for the arrival of new life. I saw, and myself benefitted from, the wide spread canopy which acted as a respite from the unrelenting rays of the summer sun. I was made privy to the intermingling of the leafy branches and an evening breeze as they spoke one to another while I sat beneath the tree on nights when I was fortunate enough to gain a few moments of solitude despite my state of confinement.

Of all of this, I was left to ask myself, "Why am I unlike this tree?" All the things I've witnessed in this tree, these things are merely the appointments of this living thing, there from its genesis; endowed by its

Creator. I too have had things appointed to me. Perhaps I am in error for even stopping to ponder this matter. Nevertheless, is it possible to grasp enlightenment from a tree?

To stand tall, to reach again towards the heavens after having been cut down by men who look upon me with an unfavorable countenance, seeing in me nothing but that I am useless, that I am merely obstruction to safety?

Then came a day that I will not soon forget. With a broken heart, resisting the urge to turn away, I watched as they mutilated your glorious canopy, as though they were instructed to perform some grotesque act of execution, and that your crown was to be decapitated. I watched as they did to this living thing what was to be done to those labeled "Obstructions." They did this all without so much as the slightest consideration that you had changed into something both beautiful and beneficial.

I have witnessed many things during my time in this place, but of them all, I've seen the most amazing thing in you oh tree. I witnessed your resilience, your ability to do the thing you were created to do—to reach heavenward while offering of yourself a living sacrifice to the welfare of others, even as still others took delight in cutting you down for their own satisfaction. I only hope; I hope for myself that before I am cut down by the sword of death, I too can be seen with the same worth as I have found in you.

ANONYMOUS KQUOTE

TAKE SOME TIME AND THINK ABOUT THIS FOR A MINUTE:

If you don't stand up for something you might just fall for whatever
and miss a chance to change a thing that's bad to that which is better

We need to learn to stick together, if we don't then we've lost
because disease, drugs, police and us is knocking us off

We talk a lot about what's wrong, what are we doing to fix it,
can't answer that, yet we're quick to come together and kick it

What I don't get is just why is it that you people don't get it,
why are you blind to the picture when it's clearly so vivid

How are you fooled by an illusion wicked people depicted,
living life like it's amusing until calamity visits

It seems now days that's the only time that family visits
because social media has now trapped all our families in it

And I could speak about this to you till I run out of breath,
but you don't hear me, like I'm talking to a people that's deaf

So what is left except to do that which I know would be best,
focus on rectifying myself and stress not over the rest

My knowledge tells me life's a test and not to focus on this world,
and that I shouldn't waste my time and to the swine cast my pearls

Or give my jewels to fools who'll never use what I have to give them,
amused that I refuse these man made rules that still imprison them

I'm far from friends with those of them that's not on the path,
some of us get and some don't, it's kind of sort of like math

In order to pass you have to pay attention in class,
before you know it you've got older, time be moving too fast

When you look back, what will you have to show for it all?
a couple cars, a house, some cash, I guess that's something to y'all

Something we all should think about is where we'll rest when it's over,
because for certain death is coming, every day it gets closer

And since yesterday passed on and today is nearly gone,
with time moving like it is, a year is really not that long

62

Have you been living right or wrong?

Have you done more good than bad deeds?

So what you grew up in the hood!

We all came up amongst some bad seeds

You aren't the only one with needs, I just know who gives provisions,
just like I know who gave me life and the reason why I'm living

I know the Truth so there's no use in trying to tell me that it isn't,
they say what separates a people is division of religion

I don't dispute the Truth in that at all, in fact I too agree
the truth can't mix with falsehood, those two will always disagree

But everybody thinks they're right, wrong nobody wants to be,
and so they fail to see what wrong with their false ideology

So you do you and I'll do me, let's just agree to disagree,
because U.N.I cannot unite, that's why there is no unity

Being black is not enough and being kin don't mean too much at all,
and we cannot unite for money because the love of it corrupts us all

The love of God engulfs us all, but still we can't see eye to eye,
because what is false looks like the truth and what is Truth today
    seems like a lie

True knowledge does exist yet most persist to live in ignorance,
claiming that they're saved, which clearly shows they need deliverance

So many people have been duped and fooled because they
    have allowed it,
so like the prisons are today, Hell will soon be overcrowded

For those who think they'll be in Heaven I say to you, I truly doubt it
because from those things of the unseen we don't know much about it

I know my vision's far from clouded, I know that Satan is quite clever,
therefore I'm standing firm on mine as not to fall for just whatever

Because if you don't stand up for something you might fall for whatever
and miss a chance to change a thing that's bad to that which is better

We haven't learned to stick together because people is lost,
that's why disease, drugs, police and us keeps knocking us off

We talk a lot about what's wrong, what are we doing to fix it?
Can't answer that still we're quick to come together and kick it

I'll never get it just why is it that some people don't get it,
blinded to the picture when it's clearly so vivid

Instead they cling to this illusion wicked people depicted . . .

Not realizing that this life on earth is merely a visit . . .
Take some time and think about this for a minute . . .

LOAN OF TIME

We take it for granted as if we have it just to waste away, as if we had a guarantee yesterday that we would awake today

It seems we just don't understand it or we can't grasp just what it really is, we use it like it's ours but it's not yours or mine, it's really His

We never seem to have enough, yet it's crazy how we let it pass, as a youth it seemed to move slow, now that I'm grown it seems to move too fast

Everybody gets their share while unaware of the amount we have, but we squander and abuse it, discard and lose it like it's merely trash

More valuable than cash and we all know how much we value that, but unlike money, once it's gone you can't earn more, nor can you get it back

A fact that most of us hardly take into consideration, giving less to the Creator and our best to the creation, then we wonder why we go through trials and tribulations

Because we take it for granted, this duration that's been loaned to us, forgetting that a loan despite how long doesn't belong to us

Yet we waste it every day on things not beneficial, like selling dope, robbing folks, gang banging, shooting pistols, preoccupied with superficial small affairs of this life

Twenty four hours in a day, we might have said a prayer twice and I'm just being nice because most of y'all don't stop to pray at all

Naaaw . . . we'd rather shoot dice, slam dominoes or play some basketball, chilling with the homies, doing that which only hinders you, prison gets real lonely, when the homies don't remember you

We always say what we intend to do but never get it done because we think just like today did, tomorrow going to come

You can tell the way we speak we must think we're in control, like we've forgot about the One in whose hand is our soul

The One who sits upon His throne, who said to worship Him alone, but we be too caught up to worship Him from worshipping our phones

We give the internet and television most of our attention and so our knowledge of this world outweighs that of our religion

I hear people every day discussing topics that are worthless and most of these people walk this earth and don't even know their purpose

So we dedicate our lives to our careers and occupations, distracted by the call of the traps and snares of Satan: technology, pornography, adultery, and fornication; love of money over God; pride, lies, and intoxication

We succumb to our desires without a pause for contemplation, that if today were you to die, what is your final destination?

We'd like to think we'd go to Heaven, for Hell is not the place to be, but see we want to go to Heaven, but we don't wanna pay the fee

Because you can't get in for free despite whatever you've been taught, having faith precedes good deeds which means to act on what you talk

Some of us don't like the Truth because it's proof against our faults, that's why every time I've came, I've brought nutritious food for thought

I could go on and be quite long but now I'm cautious what I do with mine, I'd advise you do the same and guard the way you use this loan called Time . . .

WHAT YOU DECIDE TO DO

I'm not a killer but survival makes us all do
What we have to do.
We keep dark secrets in dark, still Allah is aware
Of all we do.

It's funny how one makes look easy that which is
Complex to you
And pride is hard to swallow but not because
It's hard to chew.

Bad deeds, we do so many till our sins amount
To quite a few,
Good deeds, if we do any, it's not as many as
We ought to do.

Somewhere I read where someone said, "Beneath the sun
There's nothing new."
Today I often wonder that if what I read
They said was true.

It's crazy what someone will do just to get
Ahead of you
And people that you think you know show you a side
You never knew.

They say they keep it real, but keep it real is what
They hardly do.
But speaking it is easier than the action that's
Required of you.

Once time expires it's too late if you did what you
Desired to do.
For you can't lie to Allah the same way Satan came
And lied to you.

So get your life on track and don't look back: that's what
I'm trying to do.
If you ain't on that path I hope that path will come
In time for you.

I say this 'cause I've traveled down that road you're on
A time or two,
But freedom is the choice for you to do what you
Decide to do. . .

KIRBY LOWE

*The following collection of thoughts is a journey through the loss of a
loved one and the struggle between us and our own inner demons.
See, we more often than not ignore the things that shape our lives daily
due to the ease that brings us mentally, but, truthfully, this is as helpful
as attempting to trap sand through a sifter. Suffice it to say, the finer
pieces fall through, building a much stronger foundation for our own
failure. . . . so if you so choose, place yourself in the mind of "The
Traveler."*

INEVITABLE OUTCOMES

I fear that my coping mechanisms have become detrimental to my own downfall because this "ability" to string together $10 words distracts me from the meat of the matter which is this: I am running out of reasons to invest in this event that is my own existence because the return is centered solely around the lies I have created to allow myself to get this far in life, and I am afraid that a buyout is looming in the dark parts of my soul created from an inability to accept the things I have done. Darling, you and I live together in my mind and to me . . . he looks just like you. I need to hear your voice like a diabetic needs insulin because, after too long, this sadness builds to a brittle rage breaking off piece by piece into my veins until it rips into my heart, laying bare every pain I ineffectively hide from prying eyes, and the smile worn is becoming as substantial as your face in my mind . . . I miss you and how your hands fit perfectly in mine while your tone always calmed the anger inside . . . I feel without purpose away from you, as if my legs do not work, and I am stranded waiting for the next time we speak to alleviate this pressure building inside because I am never as happy as when I was near you, like I was made solely to be with you, that my purpose was to make you smile and laugh because no one can ever love you like I do or know you the way I have come to . . . even though this love is sick and codependent this does not change the reality of the fact that everything else is merely filler, distracting me until I have you again because . . . I just want to be loved for who I am and not who I have created. See, I fear I will never find another like you my dear because my evil and yours were one and the same, and my only true regret left in life is that I did not follow you when I had the chance.

A CARBON COPIED COLLECTIVE

I yearn to like myself the way others have come to because I acknowledge the qualities within myself that they find admirable, but unbeknownst to them those exact same traits have been meticulously copied from the perspective father figures I have encountered on my journey, but then again isn't this something we all do in some way yet continue to believe this is what creates our uniqueness? Is it how we employ this specific trait? An ability to speak in itself is nothing amazing yet there is a vast difference between MLK and Hitler. So we are all looking for something that distinguishes us from the rest, and as these ideas are given life I realize my issues are in reality no different from anyone else's, the difference lies in this overwhelming sense of introspectivity I have been cursed with. So I will continue looking for pieces of people I admire because I have no issues being a follower of good men because what are leaders without followers, if not failures.

NOTHING SAYS GOODBYE LIKE SIX FEET OF DIRT

As they stand around all dressed to impress, I am losing this fight to feeling depressed. Because you were swollen with child and bursting with so much pride, I'd never have guessed that death would be your bride. And your friends stand apart feigning shock, and I can't help but overhear them talk of claiming ignorance of what they could have done while hiding hands all covered in your blood. And they all bring you red roses, but I brought you white, and your aunt makes a scene like it's opening night. But darling for me you held center stage, a vision of health just seconds from waking, and I fool myself that you're just waiting for a kiss from prince charming to break this evil spell, and you'd open your eyes, releasing me from this hell, but your soul is gone and I'm no prince and, while I am wondering if this world will ever make sense, a man in a white collar approaches and claims in a fatherly voice devoid of any shame that he can grant you absolution to send you to Christ, and this all can be done for a reasonable price, and so now for pennies and dimes he sings your praises poetically put in eloquent phrases, and your parents try to buy their redemption by ignoring the fact that it would have only taken a little attention to keep this tragedy from ever taking place, and even now your father can't look me in my fucking face, as he halfheartedly spits venomous accusations to beat me like fists, but he doesn't understand my heart no longer exists and then, just like that, with tears in his eyes he gets up on stage and says his goodbyes, and one by one they file past, all of them saving me for last, and when it's my turn to speak my head spins and my knees grow weak and my mouth feels like it's filled with cotton and all I can utter is you'll never be forgotten by those you have loved. But I will never forgive you for what you have done. See you chose a permanent solution to whatever was wrong and for that I question whether you loved me at all, and a cynical man once said to view this as evolution in action and getting over you will be as easy as grade school subtraction, but I guess that he did not know that me minus you left nothing at all and these steps into madness turned into a fall, and while losing you was just too much leaving me more than a little out of touch, you being the one to always take more than you give took something now I can never forgive . . . you took from me the sound of a house full of the pitter patter of little feet and the music of her little heartbeat. The sight of her small hand in mine and the joy of staying up late to read her her favorite story "just one more time" . . . darling in one selfish act you stole all that from me and now my eyes fill so that I can barely see, but I take a deep breath and force a sneer because I'll never let these people see any tears, and with that I exist stage left and walk to the car and on the way I eat a few bars like a kid with a Pez dispenser even though I know it is not the answer but fuck it . . . and when I get in J___ turns to me and hands me a blunt and says to me, "Bro fuck that cunt . . . see me, Ben, and Chris are all the family you need and when you get cut man all of us bleed so why don't you lean back and take a hit to clear your mind of all this shit" and so I take his advice without thinking twice and say to myself that it would have been nice to have heard you say goodbye or at least have known why . . . And then I long to hold you to the point my bones ache and hurt because nothing says goodbye like six feet of dirt.

UNTITLED

It seems to me that the more time passes by the less I'd like to try and smile, and when interacting with people I unconsciously spit out the prerecorded messages that have had the most success to quickly interact, distract, and disengage the prospective conversationalist with practiced efficiency . . . I notice that my disdain for those around me grows daily and this pain I hide inside begins to radiate dangerously, so much that I cannot help but replay each and every violent moment in my life, so I fight the urge to display a play by play on the first person to address me incorrectly . . . I am reaching meltdown levels and this smile I project to the masses is gaining a noticeable tic at the edges while the noise in my head has reached a level of deafening distraction due to the fact that my inner enemy emits a recurring theme consisting of past failures and future regrets that seem to go unheard by those surrounding me . . . Is it selfish of me to be angered by the joy that I bring to others when I long sickeningly for the same in return because I am constantly at war with this beast inside me that is vying for my end while I try to continue this facade, carefully mastered over years of lies, and find the effort wasted and tiring . . . a pressure is building inside hoping for release and my veins seem a likely route because every attempt previous the next was merely a search for the path of least resistance and I wish that these people could see the war inside me that I am fighting but losing . . . having to see the lines pushed back year by year until all that's left is this small foxhole full of every precious memory that I hold onto to keep myself breathing, and so honestly fuck anyone who thinks this is a game or some joke or thinks that I am weak or not "manly," if only they could experience the pain that eats my soul and the headaches that rip my skull in halves revealing the thoughts that run my life? Why won't he just stop talking to me and let me live, let me be happy with the person I am becoming and stop throwing the one I once was in my face every time I look in the mirror . . . but now I realize it is because everything that I am becoming is based off of the lie that I am happier than what truly exists inside and I tire of the games played, to smile when I am sad and to laugh when I want to cry . . . I do not want to die but I feel like it is the only way this will stop . . .

KEITH CHARISMA

Keith Charisma, author and lecturer, has a devotion to exposing the plight of the families who comprise Black America. A devoted father, he commits to a style of writing that is experiential, comedic, and laced with a reality that his children can relate to and his wider audience can appreciate. He lives in Lexington, Oklahoma, surrounded by a cast of characters who are sometimes portrayed in his work.

A CONVERSATION WITH A TREE

A tree will never reach the sun, but that doesn't stop it from trying.
I lack the motivation of that tree, I'm not even lying.
I've been deceived, manipulated, and fallen victim to myself.
I know I should read the Bible but frankly that's a book I tend to leave
    on the shelf.
You see, I've always had a hard head—was never one that believed
    crap had a stink.
That hard head led me to a dungeon—isolated misery in every thought
    that I think.
But when you have no man to tell you how to be,
Trial and error become your father figures, permanently.
That's why I'm so tired—I've bumped my head for too damn long.
I might as well be honest with you; my life is a perpetual
    Mary J. Blige song.
I've asked men to help, but they just stare at me.
Guess I'll ask this old, sturdy, lifeless tree.
"How do you stand in a storm? How do you know when to bloom?
"Why is your bark so thick? Does it grow through and through?
"Who planted you in the soil—right where you are?
"Did you do this yourself or did you follow a pattern written
    in the stars?
"Your leaves have an odd shape—mutation or planned?
"And what makes you better than me—after all, you're a tree and
    I'm a man!
"I can cut you down and chop you in pieces.
"I can break your limbs—at least the ones my height reaches.
"I can join an army and be all I can be.
"All you can do is stand here and be a tree.
"Why don't you say something—or are you afraid of me?
"Defend yourself or lose my respect permanently!
"Oh, I get it. You're the type who doesn't answer what you
    consider foolishness.
"Silent, strong, reserved. Well, your silence is disrespectful,
    so I'll digress.
"Hey Tree! The wind is blowing! Duck and hide!
"And it looks like something is being hurled into your side!
"Wait a minute—why are you shedding your green turned
    brown leaves?
"And that fragrant emitting—is that from your flowers, Tree?
"Talk to me! Tell me something! A simple man is what I'm trying to be!
"The source of your strength is still a mystery to me.
"I discovered a diagram of what I think you're trying to hide,
"It shows me that you're as tall and strong as you are on top of the
    ground as on the inside.

"Your roots run deep and they hold you in place.

"They're strong and vast, full of potential, time, and space.

"A plethora of life they bring to you—and they provide the strength you
    need to bloom.

"They clutch the earth because theirs and your life depend
    on the clods.

"They do all the dirty work while you reach for the stars.

"The laws of gravity try to keep you from outer space—

"But your root system supports your ambition—what purpose,
    what grace!

"As you reach up, they reach down—you go for the sun and they chant
    'Go for it' from inside the ground.

"You have a support system of me—roots that support you and help
    fulfill your destiny."

A tree will never reach the sun but that doesn't stop it from trying.

And a strong man I'll be the day I give myself to my dreams and let my
    roots support me.

LEANN (FROM *THE DABNEY GIRLS*)

The morning was quiet and ordinary. LeAnn sat quietly in her black Mercedes SUV outside her son's school waiting to turn onto the street and continue her mundane routine. She'd already said good day to one of the men in her life. Now on to bid his father a good day. She was certain her husband of 11 almost 12 years would be in the mood for love making. It had been at least three days since they'd been intimate. Her lower extremities began to warm at the thought of sex. A crooked, almost devious smile came across her face as she thought, *I know what will get him in the mood. I'll strip off everything I have on in the garage and come in the house completely naked. That will get his motor running for sure.*

LeAnn was a very curvaceous 30 year old with caramel skin that was impeccably smooth, tight, and always fragranced with a body spray or lotion that made her presence all the more noticeable. Her hair was kinky and black with blonde tips. In high school, she'd been the most popular girl and the most hated simultaneously. She was the girl that all the guys wanted and all the other girls envied. Although she wasn't athletic, or in any of the social groups at school, her popularity was unparalleled by anyone else. Her signature was in at least 300 yearbooks from her senior year. She married her husband, Braxton Fitzgerald, shortly after completing high school. The small community they lived in was shocked. The two had never really been an item, and it was supposed that LeAnn would marry Jason Brady. They'd dated as juniors and seniors.

It was rumored that Braxton and LeAnn were secretly seeing each other and LeAnn got pregnant and that's why the marriage was so abrupt. This rumor was dispelled when the couple waited 5 years to start a family. So the rumor morphed into LeAnn being a gold digger as it was no secret that the Fitzgerald family was well off and well connected. Braxton's father was an insurance agent and also the longest serving city councilman in their community. His grandfather was a district court judge. Braxton himself, at age 31, was chief of the fire department. Despite what the town believed, LeAnn knew why she'd married Braxton. And that was good enough for her.

LeAnn pulled into the garage of her elegant English-manor styled home. She loved this home, although there was a time when she detested it. The home had been built by a wealthy retired architect who grew up in the area. Soon after its completion, he became very ill and never had a chance to move into it. When the home was placed on the market, no one in the county was interested, including the Fitzgeralds.

It was a mansion out on the bluffs of nowhere, at the end of a long county road with poor drainage. The grounds surrounding the home were undeveloped and overgrown. It was also over priced. The house stayed vacant for three years. When the owner died, the home was willed to the dead man's nephew who reduced the price sharply just to dump it off on someone else, and Braxton Fitzgerald's father bought it as an investment. He allowed his son and daughter in law to occupy it after the birth of their son, with the condition of turning the home and the grounds into a place fit for a king. They had succeeded. With the car parked in her spot, she let down the garage door, stepped up out of the car and began to pull all of her clothing off. She kept a bottle of lavender scented lotion in the glove box and applied some all over her body. After taking off her shoes, she opened the door to the house, stepped into the kitchen and called for her husband.

"Braxy, baby, are you up?"

There was no answer. The house was silent. She surveyed the room for any signs that he had been rummaging through the house.

"Brax, come on babe, time to get up."

LeAnn walked over to the refrigerator and pulled out a bowl of pasta salad. She started fixing her husband's lunch. Soon after she finished packing his lunch, Braxton emerged from the bedroom and stood at the entrance to the kitchen. He wasn't in uniform. Instead, he was dressed in a pair of khaki shorts and a sky blue Polo button down. He was stunned at seeing LeAnn in the kitchen naked. He always admired how beautiful she was naked. He took a moment to study her figure as she sheepishly grinned at him in a reveling gaze.

"I fixed your lunch to go but thought I would give you a taste of me for breakfast."

LeAnn began moving toward Braxton, exaggerating every step while gyrating her pelvis in a flirtatious and seductive manner. Just before reaching him, within arms length, she turned her back to him and bent over, making her ass cheeks clap.

"Oh, Brax, this is all for you baby. Come get it."

Braxton stood motionless as he watched his wife tease him, hoping to entice him to grab her and bend her over the countertop. At first, she thought he was taking it all in, then she realized he had an uninterested look on his face.

"LeAnn, I—" he stuttered as the words left him for a moment. "We need to talk. I was at the store about a week ago and I ran into Yolonda. We've been texting on and off ever since then. And, uh, I guess there's no easy way to say this, but, LeAnn, I think I still might be in love with this girl."

LeAnn stood up in silence, closely staring at the pattern of the tile in the floor as she lifted her head. She crossed her arms, covering her bare breast, a posture that meant she was feeling vulnerable.

"Brax, please tell me you're playing?"

"No LeAnn, I'm not. And I need some time to work these feelings out."

"What does that mean?"

"It means that Yolonda has asked me to go with her to Houston for a couple days and I told her I would. She thinks we need to sit down and work some things out and I agree. Look, it's not what you think. I'm not gonna sleep with her. We'll be in separate rooms. I need to figure this out. If I I am in love with her, you and me will sit down and work some things out when I get back. And, no matter what happens, I don't want you to leave this house. This is your home. You've turned it into one. You've made this place great. If I'm not in love with her, then I'll know that I'm in love with you."

"Braxton, have you lost your damned mind? You expect me to consent to you leaving me to go lay up with your ex and wait on you to decide whether or not you're in love with her or with me?"

"Look LeAnn, I know it sounds crazy, but—"

"Damn right it's crazy, and I don't know who's crazier; her coming up with a bullshit plan like that or you for going along with it. I can't believe you Braxton. We've been through a lot together and this is how you treat me? After 11 years? Really?"

Braxton rolled his eyes and looked toward the family room. He followed a pattern of light beaming in from a pair of French doors on the rear wall of the house.

"Braxton, I always felt you didn't love me, but I stuck by you anyway because I loved you. But, if you leave this house, you will never see me or Tyson again. Is that a risk that you're willing to take?"

"LeAnn, you know you're only here because of the lifestyle we—"

"Lifestyle? Braxton need I remind you that when I came into this family, you didn't have shit to your name and your father was about to lose his business? So, miss me with the lifestyle crap! What we have today was made possible by me putting in free work at your father's office, helping you do your college homework, and me putting all my fucking dreams in a wish book so I could help fulfill yours. So miss me with the lifestyle bull. Now, the way I see it, you married me and if you didn't love me, or you still had feelings for Yolonda, then you shouldn't have made the commitment because I believe in death do us part. Natural or otherwise."

Braxton looked pointedly at his wife. He could tell she was serious. They rarely ever fought. In fact, this was only their third fight in all their years of marriage.

"What's it going to be Braxton?"

"Lele, please give me some time. I'm confused. Seriously."

LeAnn began crying hysterically. "Don't you dare call me Lele you bastard. Get the hell out of my face. Now!"

Braxton walked into the garage and a few seconds later, started his Escalade and drove off. LeAnn fell to the floor of her kitchen, her body limp and heart fluttering with fear. Had she spent 11 years convincing herself that Braxton would fall in love with her someday, all the while he was only waiting for Yolonda to come back?

VULNERABILITY

I remember being awakened in the darkest hour of a new day. We had made love. Our chests were bare. The musk of intimacy permeated the air. Her face was disfigured and flushed, not from our shared experience, but from a painful one she was having alone.

My hand touched her lower back, "What's wrong my love?"

Her silent sobbing ruptured into vociferous wails. "Babe, I just want to know who he is."

For a moment, I shrunk away. I removed my touch. This was a jab at my manhood, I thought. I am her man. I am father to her children. I am provider for her home. If anyone she should want to know, it should be me. But here we are, in the grip of darkness and she is playing mistress to a phantom while in arm's reach of me. I touched her again, in the only other way I knew—carnally. I hoped to erase the chasm that was created by this missing man.

When the fever of night was broken, she was gone. No, not all at once; it took years. And it was late in the day when I realized the error of my ways. She wanted for herself what she had given me—fatherhood. I could be her man, her lover, the father of her babies, but I could never be her father. She wasn't expecting me to be. That night, she needed me to hold her and just be there. She was vulnerable and I missed it. So occupied with myself was I that I failed to be the one she could expose herself to. I knew her breast and the curves of her honey-colored body, but I was not acquainted with her.

It's a new day now and it arrived like all the others before it. Again, in the darkest hour, I awaken. But this time I am not misappropriating vulnerability; I'm the one who's vulnerable. There is something missing from my life and I'm sobbing quietly to see if anyone is awake to rescue me. I am searching in the dark, begging strangers who share this night with me to give me what I failed to give another. My nostrils sense not the perfume of ecstasy, but are assaulted by the odor of dying dreams, mine and those of the men who surround me. My nakedness is shame. I need not to know who my father is; I yearn for a different nature—freedom. And when the fever of this night breaks, I too will be gone, hopefully better and not bitter.

You see, here's how I missed it. She smiled as she raised her face in the warmth of the sun. She braided her hair to resemble the symbolic locks that define love. Her voice filled the hollows of cathedrals in the liturgy to the Invisible Reality of the Divine. In the late season of yesterday, she shared her body with me. But in the darkness, between the shift change of yesterday and today, she cried. She started her days in tears and ended them in smiles—a dichotomy that beguiled me. I only saw the smiles. And even when I saw the tears, I interpreted incorrectly.

How ironic that I live her life now. Time, that son of a bitch, has betrayed me by aligning our experiences to finally sync. I want to wake her and tell her I am sorry and I understand. But she is gone and only the musk of her memory remains. And to give the virtue of my vulnerability to another seems adulterous. But what am I to do? I reached for her, and the place where she laid is cold, the imprint of her silhouette is faded. So I unburden to strangers in hopes that she will hear me. Maybe we'll hold one another again. She left an intoxicating smell.

MR. WASHINGTON

My name is Norman D. L. Washington. I'm 25 years old and of African descent. I like writing, reading, and learning new things. My poetry is inspired by personal life experiences. The fact that I can share my deepest thoughts with the world through my writing personally means a whole lot to me. If I can satisfy my reader by expressing my life story through poetic form, my mission is complete.

ONE MISTAKE

Who knew you could lose so much on account of one mistake
Decisions you made at 18, can cost more at 28
My mother's face don't look the same, she's changing with age
Was man made to go roam the earth, or sit in a cage
I'm not looking for sympathy, and I'm not singing the blues
If I was I would be playing a guitar, drinking, and tapping my shoes
One mistake kept me alive, one mistake created life
One mistake and they gave him life, no mistakes and they saved a life,
Problems occur, so no one is perfect, my stomach is hurting,
The cabinets are empty like my mama's purses,
Label me a problem child I'm like my mama's burden,
No situation is wasted if you learn from your mistakes,
So when we die why do they say we're in a better place,
Are we forgiven through our actions, or maybe saved by grave,
If we repent is that enough, who really knows our fate?
Adam and Eve ate off the Tree that was our first mistake,
Having kids out of wed lock that was my worse mistake,
Legally labeled a minor, manning up to the choices we make,
I say we because there's more than me,
Plenty of us share the same story just not a voice to speak,
Sometimes we think we know it all, we need adults to teach,
Helping hands are in arm's reach, much love and peace

THE APPLE OF MY EYE

This is love at first sight at its purest form,
Thinking about this certain person makes my heart warm,
If it was up to me you would be queen of the universe,
Nations of people would supply your needs on this planet earth,
I can't give you the earth, because it isn't mine to give,
Just know I love you enough to die in order to see you live
Hearing your voice triggers emotion and your touch is soothing,
Your body gives off scents like a garden filled with flowers blooming,
To hear you moan is more pleasing than any other sound,
To lift you up is my pleasure, never to let you down,
Protecting you with my muscle, guarding you like my treasure,
Loving every inch of your body, to please you is my pleasure,
Your skin is milky chocolate, your eyes capture my soul,
Can I cook you breakfast in bed and massage you head to toe,
Waiting for a invitation I respect your comfort zone,
Even though I call you my girl your body yours to own,
To stand behind you in a mirror we look like King and Queen,
Taking walks on the beach at sun down, to discuss our dreams,
What it takes to make you smile, your command is my will,
If I was to even see you cry, I'd have the urge to kill,
To love your wife as you love yourself, that's what the Bible says,
I can picture us on a carriage happily newlyweds,
We can bury the past now and we can shove ahead,
We can have kids, buy us a house and let god handle the rest,
These words I'm holding deep inside are kind of scaring me.
But what the hell I'm just going to say it
Will you marry me?

CAN BAD MEN CHANGE?

A man who kills will keep killing, if he is never caught,
The drug addicts die for the high that's such a deadly cost,
Prostitutes selling their richly treasure for numbers very low,
On top of that, they pay a man who they barely know,
Gang bangers only shoot men of their own kind
Who taught us how to hate each other so deep inside,
Baby mama talk about baby daddy all on Maury,
The results come out the baby isn't his and she's not sorry,
America would rather waste the food, than feed
The poor, it takes a village to raise a kid,
Mama said don't leave the porch, people raping,
Kidnapping all these innocent kids,
They go to prison and get protection
That's how the system is,
Police trigger happy to kill a black man just for fun
All they gotta say is, "I feared for my life, I thought he had a gun."
Why the Hell would I have a gun I'm just a working man,
I go to church and cut yards on the side to feed my fam,
You call them law enforcement I call them the Klu Klux Klan,
Yeah you was scared not for your life, but fear of a black man,
They got away with murder once of course they'll do it again,
Because a killer never stops killing that's unless he's caught,
Are you sorry for what you did
Or sorry you got caught

LETTER TO MY DAUGHTER

Hey my love this is your daddy inmate #724
When I left, you were drinking milk and crawling on the floor
Now you're going to school, answering the phone, and
    scrambling eggs
The most beautiful and intelligent 5 year old I've ever met,
Daddy isn't doing much, cuz it's not much to do
Staying away from any trouble to make it home to you,
The reason that I'm even here is very hard to say,
A toxic mixture of bad friends, and choices turned mistakes
You're daddy's angel, you're my princess, you're my prized possession
Spending years living without you taught me a valid lesson,
Once you were born I shed tears, and I don't like to cry
The doctor started running tests, daddy was standing by,
When it was time to take you home I put you in the car
Your energy lit up the house just like a morning star
Your mother tells me you're getting older asking questions,
Of why I don't come to your birthdays, or why I'm still in prison,
If you never forgive me for leaving, I wouldn't blame you,
If my daddy left me hanging I would do the same too
The first time that you came to see me I felt like a stranger,
What have I gotten into? My question filled with anger
This wasn't even supposed to happen. We were a happy family
Your mama told me that you said I'm just your older brother's daddy.
My heart divided into pieces, my stomach felt so sick
I couldn't sleep praying to god that I could walk through brick
If they would let me go just one day to spend time with you
I would answer all of your questions, and do what you like to do.
Until that miracle happens, we may just have to wait.
Just keep obeying your mother, seems like she is doing great.

OPPOSITES ATTRACT

Am I the one to say you're right? Are you the one to prove me wrong?
The chemistry is like night and day. But even still we get along,
Nobody seems to understand, it's like you fell into my hands,
They say I can't but you say I can, my prayers are answered Amen.
The beauty of your precious soul, you're working hard to reach
    your goals,
I'm here to help in any way, let's make this money generate,
I'm street smart but you went to school, I went to prison and
    made it through,
Walked out those gates a different dude, but no one believed me
    but you,
I'll send roses to your job I hope they make you happy,
Last year we were like strangers, but this year were family,
Nothing in this world I regret except not meeting you sooner,
We fell in love at first sight, I thought that term was a rumor,
Good girls love bad guys, your blood is rushing from the thrill,
Tall guys love short girls, that's confident and keep it real,
Without you there is no me, I get the front you got my back!!
History repeats itself, I put my future in your past,
You have patience and you slow down the pace when I'm moving fast,
The only way this could have happened is if opposites attract.

SELF CRITICISM

Who are you? Do I really know you? Have we met?
We share a lot in common, but we're also opposites.
One day everything is smooth and we're on the same page.
Other days I get confused, because you're in a rage.
What's all this anger that you hold? What are you so mad about?
Yeah growing up with you was rough, I feel your pain no doubt.
But your kids are doing great the struggle is over now,
They live in a two parent home financed by two bank accounts,
We work for everything we have even if it's illegal,
The law makers are law breakers this whole country is evil,
Don't think I can't respect the hustle, you have mouths to feed,
But know the difference between what you want and what you need,
Your mother called the other day, I overheard the call,
Couldn't believe my ears you talked to mama like a dog,
That woman raised you the best she could and she sacrificed,
Call her back and tell her you're sorry man that wasn't right,
Staring dead at you in this mirror couldn't get more clearer,
You want to change but I sense fear that made me drop a tear,
These second chances are for granted we can end it here,
It's time to let go of the past because the future is near,
Man ain't you tired of watching your back and living reckless?
Man don't you know you could have never made it back home
        from Texas?
The enemy been in your bed and y'all been sharing lust,
And she lured you in with sex so she could set you up,
Man this ain't living this ain't life this is like dying death,
I'm talking to you but you're me I'm talking to myself,
Let go of pride and change your life at the least for your kids,
And pray to God in hopes of forgiveness for the shit you did . . .

CPSIA information can be obtained
at www.ICGtesting.com
Printed in the USA
FFHW011422260919
55204068-60934FF